IF YOU HAD YOUR BIRTHDAY PARTY ON THE MOON

BY JOYCE LAPIN

ILLUSTRATED BY SIMONA CECCARELLI

STERLING CHILDREN'S BOOKS
New York

HAPPY BIRTHDA

*For my family. I love you all to the Moon and back.
With special thanks to Prof. Stephen Schneider and
John Rudolph.*
—J. L.

*For Giulia and Nicolas: for their small steps
and their giant leaps.*
—S. C.

STERLING CHILDREN'S BOOKS
New York

An Imprint of Sterling Publishing Co., Inc.
1166 Avenue of the Americas
New York, NY 10036

Interior text © 2019 Joyce Lapin
Cover and interior illustrations © 2019 Simona Ceccarelli

ISBN 978-1-4549-2970-3

Distributed in Canada by Sterling Publishing Co., Inc.
c/o Canadian Manda Group, 664 Annette Street
Toronto, Ontario M6S 2C8, Canada
Distributed in the United Kingdom by GMC Distribution Services
Castle Place, 166 High Street, Lewes, East Sussex BN7 1XU, England
Distributed in Australia by NewSouth Books
University of New South Wales, Sydney, NSW 2052, Australia

For information about custom editions, special sales, and premium and
corporate purchases, please contact Sterling Special Sales at 800-805-5489 or s
pecialsales@sterlingpublishing.com.

Manufactured in China

Lot #:
10 9 8 7 6 5 4 3 2 1
01/19

sterlingpublishing.com

Cover and interior design by Irene Vandervoort

The artwork for this book was created digitally using Adobe Photoshop.

HOW AMAZING would it be to have your birthday party on the Moon?

Of course, everyone would want to come. Not just because it's the *Moon*—but who wouldn't want to ride to a party in a rocket?

You'll get to fly 40 times faster than a plane. And for most of the trip, you'll *also* get to . . .

The Moon is about 239,000 miles from Earth. Your rocket will fly you there in three days, but if you could walk there, you'd have nine more birthdays on the way!

. . . *float*!

Once your ship is coasting through space, everyone at your party will be weightless. Just unbuckle your seatbelt and you'll start to float—surrounded by party hats, presents, and your piñata!

At bedtime, astronauts have to strap themselves down so they don't float around and bump into one another!

You'll find that even the tiniest push will send you sailing through a sea of friends. You'll do somersaults in the air and have handstand contests on the walls. Some of you will even float upside down. Strangely, it'll feel the same as floating right-side up!

When you're weightless, there's no up or down. In fact, if your birthday cake floats upside down, it'll be just as safe as it is right-side up.

As your rocket gets close to the Moon, you'll want to buckle yourself in for the landing. You'll no longer float, but once on the Moon, you'll still be much lighter than you are on Earth.

Gravity holds people and things on the ground and pulls them back down after they go up. How strong a world's gravity is depends partly on its weight. The Moon is much lighter than Earth, which is one reason why it has weaker gravity.

Nobody knows for sure how the Moon was created, but we *do* know it happened when the Earth was very young.

Most scientists think that about 4.5 billion years ago, Earth collided with a world the size of Mars. The crash threw huge chunks of Earth's crust into space, and many pieces came together, forming the Moon.

Earlier in your trip, the Moon looked like a disk—but now it will fill your whole window!

You'll see hills as high as the highest mountains on Earth, valleys and flatlands, and boulders and rocks. Everything will be different shades of gray, tan, and brown. And you'll see the Moon's bowl-shaped craters everywhere.

In picking the very best spot for your party, it's helpful to know that the same side of the Moon always faces Earth. This "near side" of the Moon is the only side we can see from Earth, no matter what kind of telescope we use. In fact, until a spacecraft photographed the Moon's *far* side in 1959, we weren't completely sure what was back there. For all we knew, the place was crawling with extraterrestrials celebrating their *own* birthdays.

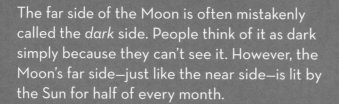

The far side of the Moon is often mistakenly called the *dark* side. People think of it as dark simply because they can't see it. However, the Moon's far side—just like the near side—is lit by the Sun for half of every month.

The near side of the Moon is where all the action is. For one thing, the Moon's near side gets *earthshine*—sunlight that's reflected from Earth onto the Moon. This reflected light shines at all times, even at night. So your party will never have to stop because it's dark out!

What's more, on this side of the Moon, you'll always have the beautiful blue Earth in your sky.

Just as Earth reflects sunlight onto the Moon, the *Moon* reflects sunlight onto *Earth*. This makes the Moon look very bright from home.

However, our planet is much bigger than the Moon, and it also reflects sunlight much better. That's why earthshine is 40 times brighter than moonlight.

When you land on your perfect party site, everyone will be eager to get out onto the Moon. But since it's your birthday, *you* get to be first! You'll climb down the ladder, followed by your friends, everybody safe in the Moon's low gravity.

HAPPY BIRTHDAY!!

You and your guests will look around in awe, hardly believing you're actually on the Moon. Then you'll look up and see Earth in your sky, many times larger and brighter than a full Moon.

Before doing anything else, you'll take seats on moon boulders and watch our planet turn. Slowly but surely, the continents will scroll by. And it'll be mind-blowing to think that everyone you know is on that globe!

However, you'll notice something very, very strange . . .

Here's a cool birthday thought:

There are about 7 billion people on Earth, but only 365 possible birthdays.* If you divide 7 billion by 365, you get around 19 million.

This means that while you're having your birthday on the Moon, 19 million other people are having a birthday on Earth!

*Not counting February 29th, which only comes once every four years.

All around you, the Moon's surface will be bright—but when you look up, the sky will be black!

To understand why the Moon's sky is black, let's explore why the Earth's sky is blue.

Light from the Sun looks white to us, but it's really made up of all the colors of the rainbow. On Earth, air causes the Sun's blue light to "scatter," and this makes our daytime sky look blue.

However, the Moon has no air—in fact, it has almost no atmosphere at all. This means there's nothing to scatter any color light at any time, and the Moon's sky is always a deep black.

An *atmosphere* is the layer of gases* surrounding a world. Earth's atmosphere is *air*, a mixture of nitrogen and oxygen.

Any atmosphere will escape into space if there's not enough gravity to "hold it down." And the Moon has so little gravity that it can't hold on to much atmosphere.

*A *gas* is an invisible form of matter, such as oxygen. Another gas is *helium*, which is often used to inflate balloons.

And now for the very best part of your Moon party: bouncing and gliding along the Moon's surface, in gravity that's only one-sixth of Earth's.

The first people who walked on the Moon, Neil Armstrong and Buzz Aldrin, said moonwalking felt like moving in slow motion. People who watched it on TV said it *looked* like slow motion!

The space program that landed the first humans on the Moon was called *Apollo*. The Apollo program began in 1961 and brought Armstrong and Aldrin to the Moon in 1969. By the time these spaceflights ended in 1972, twelve Apollo astronauts had walked on the Moon—but none of them on their birthdays!

Now it's *your* turn!

If you weigh 100 pounds on Earth, you'll only weigh about 17 pounds on the Moon. You'll find yourself leaping six times higher and farther than you can on Earth. No need for a bounce house at this birthday party!

One-handed push-ups will be easy peasy. In fact, if you push up too hard, you might push yourself right to your feet!

Throw or hit a ball on the Moon and it'll fly six times farther than it would on Earth. It'll also stay "in the air" six times longer. Hit a homerun at your party and, after running the bases, you'll have time for group photos before the ball lands!

In 1971, astronaut Alan Shepard became the first person to play golf on the Moon. In an area of the Moon called the *Fra Mauro* formation, Shepard hit two balls with a club he'd snuck onto Apollo 14. Shepard wasn't a very good golfer on Earth, but he was a great golfer on the Moon!

You'll probably be bursting to check out the Moon's craters.

A *crater* is a bowl-shaped "scar" that marks the spot where an asteroid crashed. Some craters are smaller than pinheads; others are the size of kiddie pools. And a few are big enough to be seen all the way from Earth!

Asteroids are chunks of rock and metal flying through outer space. Most of them are "leftovers" from when the planets first formed.

The majority of the solar system's asteroids crash-landed on moons and planets billions of years ago, so most Moon craters are incredibly old.

However, millions of asteroids still roam the solar system. Keep your fingers crossed that none of them crash your party!

The most remarkable thing about Moon craters, though, is that many look the same as they did when they were first created billions of years ago.

Because the Moon has no atmosphere, it also has no weather—no wind or rain to "erase" craters or other dings. This means the Moon's surface hardly changes over the years. And when it *does* change, it's because of something from another world, like *you*.

The footprints left by America's Apollo astronauts are about a half-century old. But they're still in such perfect condition that if you visited an Apollo landing site, you'd see exactly where the astronauts walked.

You might be wondering how you'll have time to do everything you want on the Moon—so you'll be happy to know that your Moon birthday will last nearly 30 days!

How does the Moon deliver this mega-birthday?

Well, like Earth, the Moon *rotates* (spins like a wheel). Each full rotation equals a single day.

Earth takes 24 hours to rotate, so one day on Earth is 24 hours. But the Moon takes 709 hours to rotate—that's 709 hours of birthday!

24 HOURS   709 HOURS

When you're ready for a different kind of playground, you can visit the Moon's *maria*.*

Maria are the parts of the Moon that look dark from Earth. Scientists used to think these dark areas were oceans, so they named them maria, which means "seas." Almost one-third of the Moon's near side is maria, but hardly any of the far side is. (Nobody is sure why.)

The Moon's maria formed billions of years ago. In those days, the Moon had hot, melted rock called *lava* inside it.

Scientists think that very large asteroids crashed into the Moon, cracking its surface. Lava then flowed out onto the Moon and hardened, creating the smooth, dark maria we see today.

* *Maria* (pronounced *MAH-ria*) is plural. The singular for maria is *mare* (pronounced *MAH-ray*).

The Moon's flat maria would be a perfect place to play freeze dance—*if* you could hear music on the Moon, which you can't.

Sounds can only travel through a *medium*, a substance like air or water that fills up the space between objects. The Moon's surface doesn't have anything like this, so there's no way for music or other sounds to reach you.

A game of freeze *tag* would be a better choice. But because low gravity makes sudden stops tricky, it's hard to know what freeze *anything* would be like on the Moon!

What will happen to the balloons at your birthday party?

Well, balloons can only fly when they're lighter than the air around them. That's why people fill them with lighter-than-air gases, like helium. But since there's no air on the Moon, balloons are too heavy to fly there. In fact, if you dropped a balloon and a moon rock together, they'd fall to the Moon's surface at exactly the same time.

The good news is you'll never have to worry about your balloons flying away!

And now for something you can't do anywhere but the Moon: Find the weird stuff the Apollo astronauts left behind!

Some things were left on the Moon for a reason. Others were left there simply because it was easier. Here are just a few "goodies" for your birthday scavenger hunt:

Six American flags, faded to white, since the Moon's ultra-thin atmosphere can't block the Sun's rays. These flags are held open by wire, because the Moon has no wind to make them wave!

12 pairs of space boots

A four-leaf clover

A falcon feather

Astronaut Shepard's two golf balls

A very rude drawing (this one might be just a rumor!)

A moon buggy

FROM PLANET EARTH

JULY 1969

A recorded message from the Queen of England and other world leaders

Movie magazines

One thing you'll love about roaming the Moon is the nice squishy cushion of dust under your feet.

This soft carpet of moondust—two inches thick—might tempt you to lie on your back and make "moon angels." Go right ahead! Remember, the Moon doesn't "refresh" its surface. So if you ever return for another birthday, your moon angels will still be there!

Dust on the Moon acts differently from dust on Earth.

When dust or light soil is kicked up on Earth, air rubs against it, slowing it down. This *air resistance* makes the dust seem to "float."

But since there's no air on the Moon, there's no air resistance, and dust returns to the ground much more quickly. Before anyone can say "Happy Birthday!" the dust churned up by your party games will be gone.

All of your guests will surely want to pick up a nice moon rock to bring home. A light-colored rock will probably be from a hill or a crater. A dark-colored rock might be from the Moon's maria.

Whichever rock you pick, just make sure it's small. A rock you can lift easily on the Moon is going to weigh six times more back on Earth!

It's getting close to that wonderful time when you blow out your birthday candles and make a wish. There's one small problem, though: Candles won't light without air.

There's air inside your rocket, but you won't want to waste it on candles. Anyway, what could you wish for that beats a birthday party on the Moon?!

Candles or no candles, it's back to your rocket for pizza and cake. Inside, there's enough air for everyone to take off their space helmets—and for you to be able to hear them sing "Happy Birthday!"

In 2001, Pizza Hut delivered pizza to the International Space Station. So maybe they'll also deliver to the Moon! If you get what the Space Station astronauts got, you'll have a large cheese pizza with extra spices and salami.

You'll probably want to have fruit punch with your pizza. But the Moon's low gravity will make pouring so slow that you may want to start filling cups before you're thirsty!

Since you're on the Moon, why not eat your birthday cake like an astronaut? Chocolate-pudding cake squeezed from a foil pouch is a Space Station favorite. After all, you don't need a place for candles!

If there's one thing you probably never expected to do, it's hit a piñata on the Moon.

To swing a piñata stick in low gravity, you'll need to plant your feet firmly on the ground. In fact, the winner is likely to be the person who can stay on their feet while swinging.

When the piñata breaks, the prizes will drop very slowly. Everyone will have time to see where their favorite treats are going to land!

Because piñata prizes will fall slowly on the Moon, they'll also spread out much farther. You'll have candies and chocolates in every corner of your rocket!

But don't worry that these treats will be lost. The minute your rocket returns to outer space, the prizes will start floating, ready to be grabbed!

There's no better way to wrap up your Moon party than with a glorious rocket ride home.

You and your friends will have three days in space to open your presents, chase floating piñata prizes, and rip into goodie bags stuffed with Moon pies. You'll probably also look back at the Moon and try to find the exact spot of your party.

As Earth gets larger and larger in your window, you'll wish your Moon party didn't have to end. But hopefully—very, very soon—you'll all be invited to someone *else's* birthday on the Moon!

YOU'RE INVITED
TO A

BIRTHDAY
PARTY!

ON TITAN

THAT'S SATURN'S LARGEST MOON

How to Get There:

Titan →

Earth

Saturn

GLOSSARY

AIR The mixture of gases in Earth's atmosphere

AIR RESISTANCE The slowing effect that's created when a light object rubs against air

APOLLO The series of space flights that first brought people to the Moon

ASTEROID A space rock that orbits the Sun but isn't big enough to be called a planet

ASTRONAUT A person trained to participate in space flights

ATMOSPHERE The layer of gases surrounding a world; Earth's atmosphere is *air*, a mixture of nitrogen and oxygen.

CRATER A bowl-shaped "scar" that shows where an asteroid crashed

EARTHSHINE Sunlight that's reflected off Earth and onto the Moon

EXTRATERRESTRIAL Someone or something that's separate from Earth

FAR SIDE The side of the Moon that always faces *away* from Earth

GAS An invisible, air-like substance that can expand to fill any volume or shape

GRAVITY A force that "pulls" people and objects toward the ground

HELIUM A gas that weighs less than air; helium is often used to inflate balloons.

INTERNATIONAL SPACE STATION An astronaut work station about 250 miles above Earth

LAVA Hot, melted rock that can flow like a river

MARIA The dark areas of the Moon that can be seen from Earth; *maria* (pronounced *MAH*-ria) is plural, and the singular is *mare* (pronounced *MAH*-ray).

MARS The fourth planet from the Sun; Mars is about half as wide as Earth.

MEDIUM (used as a noun) A substance, such as air or water, that fills the space between objects

MOON An object that orbits another, larger object in space

MOONLIGHT Sunlight that's reflected off the Moon and onto Earth

NEAR SIDE OF THE MOON The side of the Moon that always faces toward Earth

NITROGEN One of the gases that make up air

ORBIT To move in a path around another object

OXYGEN One of the gases that make up air

PLANET A large, round object that orbits a star

SOLAR SYSTEM A star (such as our Sun), plus all the planets and objects that orbit it

(THE) SUN The star at the center of our solar system

SELECTED BIBLIOGRAPHY

Barbree, Jay. *Neil Armstrong: A Life of Flight*. New York: Thomas Dunne Books, 2014.

Branley, Franklyn M. *The Moon Seems to Change*. New York: HarperCollins Children's Books, 1960 and 2015 (revised edition).

Buckley Jr, James. *The Moon* (Smithsonian). New York: Penguin Young Readers, 2016.

Cain, Fraser. "Gravity on the Moon." *Universe Today*, updated December 24, 2015. universetoday.com/19710/gravity-on-the-moon.

Donnelly, Judy. *Moonwalk: The First Trip to the Moon*. New York: Random House, 1989.

Dunford, Bill, Celeste Hoang, Elizabeth Landau, and Jay R. Thompson. "First Photo of the Lunar Far Side." *NASA Science*, updated September 26, 2017. moon.nasa. gov/resources/26/first-photo-of-the-lunar-far-side/.

Scott, Elaine. *Our Moon: New Discoveries About Earth's Closest Companion*. New York: Clarion Books, 2016.

Simon, Seymour. *The Moon*. New York: Scholastic, 1984; and Simon & Schuster, 2003 (revised edition).

Stewart, Melissa. *Meteors* (National Geographic Kids series). Washington, D.C.: National Geographic Partners, LLC, 2015.

Wilkinson, Philip. *Spacebusters: The Race to the Moon*. New York: DK Publishing, 1998; and Turtleback Books, 2012.

SUGGESTIONS FOR FURTHER READING

Abbott, Simon. *100 Questions About Outer Space*. New York: Peter Pauper Press, 2018.

Bennett, Jeffrey. *Max Goes to the Moon: A Science Adventure with Max the Dog*. Colorado: Big Kid Science, 2012.

DePrisco, Dorothea. *Discovery Spaceopedia: The Complete Guide to Everything Space*. New York: Liberty Street (Time Inc. Books), 2015.

Editors of *TIME for Kids* magazine. *X-Why-Z Space*. New York: TIME For Kids Books, 2014.

Floca, Brian. *Moonshot: The Flight of Apollo 11*. New York: Atheneum/Richard Jackson Books, 2009.

Kluger, Jeffrey. *To the Moon!* New York: Philomel Books, 2018.

Priddy, Roger. *Space*. New York: Priddy Books, 2018.

Siy, Alexandra. *Footprints on the Moon*. Massachusetts: Charlesbridge, 2001.

Stott, Carole. *Night Sky*. New York: DK Publishing, 1993 a

Thimmesh, Catherine. *Team Moon: How 400,000 People Lo Boston, New York: HMH Books for Young Readers,